DEEP ROOTS

Illuminations in Etymology

Frank Marrero, *Enelysios*

Copyright © 2016 Frank Marrero. All rights reserved
Tripod Press
61 Tamalpais Road
Fairfax, California 94930
www.frankmarrero.com
ISBN: 0-9673265-4-0

Tripod Press

Table of Contents

Notes:

From Greece to Hellas 7
Writing on the Wall 8

Part One: Contemplations and Rhapsodies

Thinking and Thankful 11
Civility 13
Same Old, Same Old 16
Character 18
Attention! 22
Conscious 25
The Yoga of Religion 26
Metanoia 27
Sophia 30
A Theory of Theatre and Theology 32
Understanding Sublime 33
Human 36
Heresy 38
Iota 39
Heart Feeling 42
Get Real? 44
Truth 46

Part Two:

The Error of Belief 51
Epilogue: Heraklitos Redux 63
Also by Frank Marrero 65
About the Author 66

*Fools are those who are not in constant intercourse
with their own nature.*

- and -

Fools are those who do not understand their own language.

— Heraklitos "the Obscure", 2500 years ago

Notes:
From Greece to Hellas

At no time in any of its history did the Hellenes refer to their country as "Greece", to themselves as the "Greeks", nor their language as "Greek." This mistake has been proposed to be a very early Latin error whereby the initial encounter with the Hellenes was via one town Graia, "Gray", on the coast of Boestia. This blunder can be likened unto Columbus insisting he had indeed discovered India and thus the Natives of the New World have been referred to as "Indians" ever since. Therefore, like "Peking" to "Beijing" and "Bombay" to "Mumbai", I defer the name of the county and people to those who live there: the county, Hellas; the people, Hellenes. However in referring to the language, *Hellenika* is not as simple and clear as the Latin "Greek" so deference is afforded to this historical convention.

Originally Hellas indicated only the province that held the Oracle at Delphi, but because of the far-reaching desire to partake in that holy ground, the name Hellas grew to include the whole region.

Writing on the Wall

Deep Roots aspires to be a different kind of text, combining academic research, Orphic theology, and spiritual understandings from around the globe and across the ages. These spirited rhapsodies and radical understandings can be difficult at times as *Deep Roots* does not follow the conventional pattern of merely conveying information, but rather serves to create a space for open-ended contemplations.

Part One: Contemplations and Rhapsodies

Thinking and Thankful

The foundational texts of the ancient Hellenes came to pass via an itinerant blind man, who travelled from place to place at the rebirth of literacy, reciting the ancient lore: *The Illiad* and *The Odyssey*. While much of the human condition is conveyed and communicated by Homer's poetic brilliance therein, it could be argued that both texts turn upon the strategic cleverness of Odysseus. For after the armies endured nine years of stalemate, it was Odysseus who proposed the ruse of the Trojans' own symbolic animal, the horse. For the mind that is embedded in mythic understanding can be manipulated by the clever, thinking mind. Ah! There's the rub! For while strategic cleverness wins the battle of power, its hubris makes an odyssey out of going home and resting in thankfulness.

Long ago, "think" and "thank" were confluent — both in the Proto-Indo-European vocabulary (hereafter PIE) as *tong*, "to feel and think", and in Old English as *thanc*, "a grateful heart". Thinking and thanking have been one word, not two.

What you think about is what you give your heart to — in some way or another, eh? And when you memorize poems or lyrics or scripture, it is said you know them "by heart," yes?

However, as we identify with the verbal portion of the brain, the mind seems to spin off, seems to separate from the feeling core, and becomes capable of a strategic logic that is outside the heart. This is what the ancient Hellenes called *hubris* (the arrogance inherent in point of view) and *hermartia*, literally "to miss the mark", medievally translated as "synne", or sin.

The torturous mind, the hell of mentality, and the identification with the thinking stream as if inside the head behind the eyes is only liberated when the schism of thinking and thanking are rectified. If thinking is to be more than abstraction and its accompanying alienation, the mind must fall [back] into the heart. Thinking must become strong in thanking if it is not going to run on automatic all the time. It's not a great idea that quiets the mind, but stability in gratitude and appreciation, in receiving love and resting in the heart.

Think of all the wisdom about counting your blessings, being grateful, being thankful. For when the mind yields to heart-appreciation and heart-adoration, we find dear wise friends and live with an economy of thoughts in the abundance of thanksgiving.

Civility

If you investigate the word "city", you will find it has roots in the Latin *civitas*. *Civitas* is how ordinary people should treat each other in an urban setting: with civility. City is rooted in civility, indeed.

Interestingly, the deepest etymological root of "civil" (PIE *kei-* "dear, beloved, home") is also the deepest root of the Sanskrit *Siva*. *Siva* (pronounced Shiva) is Hinduism's primary god of both pure consciousness and death.

Si can be heard in hiss, hush, dissolve, and silent and *va* can be found in voice, voluntary, vote, vow. Si-va. The awareness of self-dissolution is spontaneously followed by the voice of self-awareness. Si-va, Siva, civil, cities, citizen, civilization. Fellow citizens! We die, and we have voice. Let us speak the blessings of civility.

Adi Da tenderly underscored this truth:

So let us not be stupid and cruel people. Let us be a little more humorous and loving, and acknowledge our friends compassionately. All of them are fleshily presented and dying. All of our women friends, all of our men friends—everyone who lives is dying and is confronted with the most incredible circumstance. All are deserving of our love and compassion, and also of our demand for the discipline of love beyond self-possession, so that they too can enjoy the Intuition of this happiness.

And our happiness depends on the total inspection of this life. So let us not pretend that we exist in a Disney world of beauty. This life is many-sided, and we do not know what it is. Let us recognize the situation we are in and become strong on the basis of this observation, so that we may be lovers and friends. Let us acknowledge this terrible circumstance and be happy, and stop placing stupid obligations on one another. We exist in a place that is open-ended, an edge to Infinity, and we are dying. The only way we can comprehend this complication is by sacrificing it and becoming lovers and friends.

What is it to be a citizen with a home? How did civilization (siva-lization?) come to evolve from merely organic and lively matter?

Over eons of time upon this blue-green earth, a rich organic soup became more and more refined, more and more sensitive, evolving into subtlety and complexity within a vast light-life field for billions of years. As the sunlight numinosity grew more complex, noticing sharpened, developing tools, until *the conscious contemplation of death bolted awareness to self-reflection*, and thus man and woman to language and consequent knowledge. Having tasted of the tree of knowledge, man and woman, *as man and woman*, stepped from the ocean of living energy and mysterious awareness even as we are always only simultaneous with it.

Self-death different from embedded-life is the origin of understanding. Knowledge of the limit of death defines us exactly. This awareness of mortality flashed a thunderbolt in the pre-historic dark sky, sparking dearest being and civility in primordial man and woman. I die, therefore I am.

It is said that the Yaqui shamans carry death on their left shoulder and so rightly size what they encounter. Knowledge of death carves the arc of discrimination and gives us inherent knowledge of soul and compassionate civility.

Same old, same old

To idio is Greek for "the same". An idiom poetically says the same thing as another prosaic representation; someone who doesn't understand the sameness and differences might be some kind of idiot. Do you catch my drift?

In ancient Rome, actors projected their voices through large masks, the famous Comedy and Tragedy faces. The sound (*sona*) came through (*per*) the masks: *per-sona*. These

masks (like many cultured sophistications) came from the Hellenes, but the Athenians called the actors on the stage *hypokrites*.

Hypokrites is rooted in the PIE *krei-* "to sieve, distinguish, discriminate, decide. With *hypo-* under/below, *hypo-krites* is often translated as "play a part, pretend" but carrying the intent of a back and forth explanation, like actors between and below their masks conveying an understanding. Indeed, *Krei-* is also the root of the Greek *krienesthai*, "to explain". To slowly sieve, to shift back and forth between masks, was how golden nuggets/ideas could be winnowed and explained, how a sudden discernment (L. *cern* "to sift, separate, distinguish.") could be revealed.

Originally, the masking was known, the role understood. But when the role or mask is unseen, there in no self-understanding and character or ethos is compromised. We call someone hiding behind a psychological mask a hypocrite, without deep ethics and lacking self-understanding. Are all persons hypocrites or only those without character?

In Latin there was an idiom, idem et idem, literally "over and over", but meaning "the same". Welcome to the "radical" or root understanding of "identity". We assume an identity based on a certain repetition. More than saying "I am female, male, religious, rational, national, artist, employee, sports fan, good/bad person, et cetera, over and over, we identify with our sense of separation. That identity would describe our common idiocy, now wouldn't it?

What *is* identity? Are we known (even to ourselves) by our repetitive idiosyncrasies? And indeed, what is a person? Is "All the world a stage and all the men and women merely players"? Is it possible to turn out of the sameness of our routine presumptions and assumed necessities into a greater reality?

Character

There is an entire section in *The Tibetan Book of the Dead* that gives detailed and complex instruction for yet-to-be-born souls in the nether-worlds on how to most auspiciously choose a new uterus for your rebirth (a womb with a view). Seeing a moral and devout twosome making love is best but if you can't find a couple with great virtue as they intercourse, at least find two people who are utterly given up to their joining. Yeah baby.

Many religious conceptions of the afterlife often include the pre-life and rebirth. Christians resurrect, Indians reincarnate, etc. Like Tibetan Buddhism, the Hellenic conception of rebirth is also quite nuanced and complex as it turns upon one's characteristic play with the Fates.

According to Orpheus, at some point in the endless grey afterlife or eternal celebration of Elysium, the psyche is at last enjoined within the harmony of the spheres and prepares to take birth. In accordance with the soul's character, the Fate Lachesis comes to him or her and attaches to the soul an appropriate spirit or *daimon*. Lachesis' daimon then blesses one's journey to life and then through it. Think of the Lachesis-spirit as your guardian angel (not as a pagan *demon*).

Upon the first breath (*psychein*, "to breathe"), the Three Fates, Clotho, Lachesis, and Atropos, convene around the babe. First, all of the threads that surround the new-born — the mother, the father, the country, the times, the stars, et cetera — are spun by Clotho. That was called our "spindle destiny", the multi-dimensional inheritance of how we are woven and constituted: how we look, feel, re-member, and think in context. Thus, this is the fabric of how we tend to *react*.

Next, Lachesis measured the material and apportioned how much was to be woven for each person. Inevitably, Atropos, "she who cannot be turned", cuts the fabric to its fated death.

Of the three Fates, only Lachesis is malleable. Besides any esoterics of choosing a womb, the psyche is subject to Clotho as she weaves the threads that surround us at birth. Atropos, lit. "without turn", is likewise inflexible as death demands our submission. But Lachesis is called by our own character, which is within our power to change. Many argue that a person doesn't change across a lifespan, but that would make all wisdom teaching and spiritual instruction mute, which it is not. We can deepen our character.

At the dawn of *philosophia*, Heraklitos "the Obscure" (fl. 500 B.C.E.) wrote one manuscript, supposedly a single scroll of highly nuanced maxims. Perhaps he is best remembered by "You can't step into the same river twice." (His delineations on "fools" are the lead quotes on the inside cover of this text.)

Heraklitos is also well known by "A man's character is his fate." But this translation, while conveying a great depth of understanding, was uttered with fewer words and more meaning: *ethos anthropos daimon* / character person fate. There is a causation implied by the order of the words, but

Heraklitos left out any verb, acausally presenting his jewel of wisdom with a suggested singularity. The logic of the psyche dictates the psychologies of the individual and simultaneously summons the pattern of experience. Our archetypical patterns not only configure the development of our psyche, it is likewise imprinted upon the flow of time by our *characteristic* choices.

Heraklitos presumed his listeners would be familiar with the Orphic description of the Underworld, the processes of rebirth, and with the three Fates. He presumed his audience knew that Lachesis is called by the character of the soul and blesses each character with a helping spirit; Heraklitos spoke to listeners who knew this Fate is not inflexible but rather gracious; she is known for her blessing disposition. With these mythological features of Lachesis as foundational knowledge, Heraklitos clarified prosaically that we can rationally see how our character calls our fate. *Ethos anthropos daimon.*

When asked "Are the stars causative?" the great sage Plotinus referred to the teaching of the Fates, assigning the astrological thread to the Spindle Destiny of Clotho. Plotinus asserted that we must indeed be aware of the many threads of our cloth, but he concluded that in every moment you have a choice: you can live your Spindle Destiny and be bound to re-act unconsciously, or if you actively engage in deepening your ethos, you can exceed the re-active cloth of your birth and *respond* in feeling with maturing authenticity. Ethically empowered, we move beyond the re-activity of our cloth to the response-ability of deeper character and present feeling. Thus we live beyond automatic destinies.

Ethos, "ethical appeal", is likened unto *charisma* with its attractive shine, and is often translated as "character", which we get from another Hellenic word, *kharakter*, "imprint/mark on the soul". (Also *kharassein* is "to engrave".) In turn, the PIE root is *gher-*, to scratch or scrape. Upon each soul is scratched or engraved a "defining quality", their *kharakter*. And deepening your character gives the shine of *ethos*.

Ethos anthropos daimon. The character of a person calls / is their fate. Want a better fate? Simple. We need only to attend to wisdom and change toward stronger ethics as we deepen our character. In doing so, the graven marks upon our soul will slowly be undone in the swell of blessing; and blessings will fall upon our path and whisper into our listening.

Attention!

The only reason I didn't flunk high school Latin was that a major portion of our grade was etymology. We had to find as many words as possible from each week's vocabulary. I literally flunked every other section of the course, but I had a devoted attention for etymological studies and so aced that section. Each week, I found long and varied lists based on each word. I passed Latin with two years of straight C–'s.

A standout in my favorite etymologies was the forms of teneo, tendere, tentendi, tentus/tensus, "to stretch". To stretch before is a pretense or pretending, to stretch to fragility is tender, to stretch an offer of money is to extend another kind of tender, and to stretch your mind toward (ad-) something is to attend to it with attention.

Deeper still, we find *ten-* "stretch" also in tendere, to hold, and when your attention is held, that's *enter-tain-ment*. Zippity do Da!

Certainly we must grow our capacity for attention if we are to be not only successful, but also stably mature. Like any other muscle we tense over and over, we must exercise and stretch our capacity for strengthening our "attention muscle". Every accomplishment is grounded in the labor of focused attention.

[If our children are not involved in a growth of focus, of holding and sharpening their attention, and spend too much time having their attention held (entertainment), then, well, the zombie apocalypse is here.]

Focused light from a glass lens can create fire, focused energy in a person attends to a host of human fires. Consider that the Latin word *focus* was used into the 17th century as the common word for "hearth", the fiery point of convergence for the home.

It is also worth noting that while the sexual attraction for propagating the species commands great amounts of our hot attention, we only have attention for sex once we're sure we're not going to die. Only after he is safe at last does James Bond get the lover, yes?

Speaking of attention, sex, and stretching, the Hindu word for sexual yoga is *tantra*, originally meaning "loom", and is also rooted in the same PIE root *ten-*, stretch. The loom holds the stretched threads for the attendant weaving of the fabric. When lovers weave in and out of each other, weave penetrating and penetration, weave two and One, this yoga is called *tantra*.

But attention does not just make for great accomplishment and tantric conductivity, there is an unseen tension in attention (and tantra). Tension is at the root of attention, both linguistically and existentially. Usually, we just presume to have attention, and just like we don't usually think about thinking, we rarely notice the tension at the root of attention. (No wonder the news is bad; attention is formed from a tension.)

Is there a dimension or function or maturity that can be unguardedly aware of our fundamental anxiety, concern, and dissatisfaction? What is the fundamental tension? From the

Buddha's *dukkha* to the existential angst of the modern mind, this deepest tension is a most profound inquiry. Certainly, this enlightenment is beyond the scope of this text and author, but each of us can come to utterly accept our every feeling.

When our anxious tension is not clothed in the objects of attention and every desire is un-resisted and naked, dark feelings graciously morph into the richness of feeling itself. This is *sadhana*, or spiritual work, the labor we gratefully learn and practice.

But when we are not in a state of grace, we live as if separate. We are going to die. We are afraid, and we'd better pay attention. But concern about concern is just more, uh, concern. Therefore, we must not only develop our capacity for attention, we must also develop our capacity to recognize, accept, and relax the inner tension. We mature by both holding on and letting go; we grow in focus and intent as well as gratitude and trust.

We let go of trying to get attention and stretch ourselves to receiving and giving attention. We labor to develop free attention, that natural awareness that is possible when life's tasks are sufficiently addressed. Indeed, "school" is rooted in the Greek *sklohe*, "leisure." With free attention, we not only learn new things, we eventually grow beyond the confinement of the verbal mind. My friend Raul loves to say, "The thinking mind is a great servant and terrible master".

Adi Da taught the cultivation of free attention, beginning with ordinary human responsibility, and upon this foundation, the contemplation of native joy. In such rest or grace, we can even notice the stream of thoughts and the tension in each one, seeking for joy. We may notice how every thought is stretched across an unseen tension, hung upon the armature of attention. Witnessing the previously unseen tensing is a revelation, the beginning of radical responsibility.

We can learn to not only focus and discern, but also to let go of the concern and tensing that is the hub and spoke of every thought. We can begin to do this as we cease to interfere with the free awareness, native luminosity or conscious-ness that is tensed to make attention. Our primal identity is found in this protective tensing.

Intrinsically recognizing and releasing the inner tensing, we trust to ground, we enter the company of the immortal beloved, we behold the beauty of what is most real, and attention/identity dissolves at last in the singularity of being.

The Yoga of Religion

It's not muscles that connect and hold our bones together, but rather ligaments. "Ligament" is rooted in the Latin *ligare*, "to bind or connect". Tear your ACL and you want it reconnected right away.

Now if you are feeling disconnected from others, everything, and even yourself, you want and need the feeling of connectedness. That's *re-ligare*, religion. Just like no one complains about rebinding a ligament, no one should complain about real religion. Real religion is not objectionable myth nor provincial dogma; "religion" is that which serves the feeling of connectedness.

An etymological cousin of the Hindi "yoga" is the English "yoke", also meaning to bind or connect. In India, yoga is to connect or bind oneself to the Divine. Original religion is the same as original yoga: to connect to the fundamental reality, to yoke ourselves to the Wholeness that reveals itself to be divine.

Conscious

"Conscious" is Latin in origin; *con-*, "with" plus *scire*, "to know". *Scire* is also the root of that growing body of knowledge called "science". Of course, "conscience" fits perfectly here as well.

Scire's deepest root is the PIE root *skei-* "to cut or split", illuminated well via an etymological cousin, "shed". As rain is split off, the shed cuts a dry difference. This cutting discrimination delineates the form of knowledge and science.

In India we find the sword of discrimination or *vivek*. The bliss of discernment was certainly demonstrated by the aptly named, "Swami Vivekananda."

We cut through myth and make science. We even cut through science and purely enquire, abandoning knowledge like yesterday's newspaper. As we mature in cutting through all forms of knowledge, we graciously and mysteriously find ourselves within the formless shine that illuminates every yes and no, every dream and every awakening. This mysterious state of un-tensed awareness, both within and everywhere, is called "consciousness" itself.

The sages agree: Consciousness becomes stable as we exercise discrimination, discernment, and the illumination of our unconscious and subconscious scripts. A lifetime dedication to uncover every limitation is needed. Self-understanding has always been the eternal requirement for eternal awareness.

We may seek for solutions, we may resolve to grow, we may pray for dissolution in God, but beyond the world of changes is the ab-solute and formless consciousness and luminosity that informs our every thought and witnesses every state. Absolute consciousness is beyond birth and death, beyond all solutions, transcending every event as it informs every moment.

Consciousness itself is not a further abstraction, as if we could mentally package awareness (just a few gold coins away), but is the native brightness that inherently shines when we cease to cover it.

Metanoia

Metanoia is a philosophical term we get from the ancient Hellenes, usually translated as "changing one's mind" and connoting the transformation that comes with a conversion. However, to fully appreciate this most meaningful word, it behooves us to see how the ancients used it.

The ancient Asklepian healing process included medicines (*pharmacia*, "spells against death"), surgeries, theatre, cleanliness, warm waters, and the laying on of hands. But it was noted that all of these healing arts together would not make a lasting healing unless the root of one's unease or unconsciousness was turned about. The disposition of unease that called the disease had to be seen and transformed to a disposition of brighter understanding. This was metanoia.

First, the usual medicines and care were given time to effect the initial healing. Following the pharmacia, massage, and rest, a specially trained priest would converse with the pilgrim about his/her dreams, for dreams provided an unguarded way for the priest of healing to see the naked psyche and archetypical choices of the patient. Seeing the "wrong views" of the patient, the priest reflected them to the supplicant. When this clarity was received, the priest proposed "right views" that also fit. Seeing the error together with views of responsive engagement allowed the patient to turn to the positive, harmonious approach and understanding. This was metanoia.

To seal the change, the final ceremony was for the patient to actually sleep in the Room of the Divine, the Temple of the God. This practice had been known for over two millennia, most notably from Imhotep of Egypt. The Hellenes called it "Temple sleep" and described it by saying that young children naturally enjoy it. Metanoia gives us the ground to lay our pillows and rest our heads in a deep trust.

Meta- "beyond, above" plus *noia* or *nous-* "lighted awareness, mind, consciousness" gives us metanoia: Go beyond your usual way of looking at things. The Asklepian priests were clear: unless the wrong views were "gone beyond" with right views, the illness would return. Therefore, the key to the deepest healing was this simple self-understanding and turning to a brighter understanding. Metanoia.

My favorite verse from the Christian scripture also is centered upon a form of metanoia: *legon metaneite engliken gar e basileia ton ouranon,* or "Change your ways (of seeing and living) and the estate of heaven is before you." The King James translation is, well, still medieval: "Repent, the kingdom of heaven is at hand."

"Repent" comes to English via the Old French, rooted in the Latin *re-*, "turn from, against" plus the Latin *poena*, "pain"… from the Greek *poine*, "penalty"). "Re-pent" means to turn against pain. "Repent" is a terribly inadequate translation of the original metanoia, for although much of the message of right living is conveyed, "repent" has been draped in pain, guilt, and regret for so many centuries that the potency of its message is compromised.

Regardless of translation, metanoia calls. Like the Buddha touching the earth, suddenly there is paradise before you.

A Theory of Theater and Theology

I remember being enthralled in Miss Elderkin's fourth grade science class as she explained how the eye and seeing work. Upon the chalkboard she drew light from the sun bouncing off of a stick figure and going into a large eyeball (for showing how the lens inverts the figure upon its retina). Then, in an attempt to glorify scientific knowledge, she commented, "Isn't science great that we know this? Over two thousand years ago, the smartest man in the world, Aristotle, said that you see when light comes out of your eye! How silly is that?"

I was thrown into a sudden contemplation. Wait a minute: If those ancient people had any idea that someone *was* the smartest person in the world, surely he would know that if you were in a closet or a cave, you could not see. That Aristotle fellow must have been talking about something else.

When an outlier appears, it demands a deeper contemplation until a new, more inclusive conception embraces the differences. This deep contemplation was called *theoria*, rooted in *thea*, a view, a seeing. Is it just a theory or is every new theory is a new seeing, a new appreciation? Obviously, we must strengthen our capacity for contemplation.

Thea is also the word for "goddess", the feminine of *theos*, the word for "gods" and "divine". Gods, goddesses, and divinities are primarily characterized by *athanatos* or deathlessness.

I read that Aristotle spoke of the divine *theos* as "the same in a flower, a sunset, and the recognition between friends." We can glimpse the divine *theos* as well as some of its logic. *Theos-logos* demands appreciative seeing and deep contemplation; theology speaks of the wisdom thereof.

Which brings us to *thea*-tre, the viewing place, the seeing place. Original theatre was transmitted by parabolic metaphor, hung upon the Dionysian transformation of the coarse goat into the god of ecstasy. Theatre teaches us to turn from pleasures to ecstasy, from tragic fate to blessings, from passive looking to engaging seeing. Metanoia comes from the seeing place. True Thea-tre.

But seeing, *thea*, and seeing the divine goddess, *thea*, is not mere looking, not mere passivity, not the reflected images on the back of the eyeball. *Thea* is to see the primal light and presence-beauty in each and all. You delight, appreciate, intercourse with your eyes and the essence in all you see. Indeed, you see when light comes out of your eyes and you appreciate and participate in reality, liberated from the world of things by the vision of deathless beauty. *Thea thea.* I see the goddess and constant intercourse calls. Behold this divine reality.

Sophia

Sokrates loved etymology. He wanted to know what was meant by words as well as their lineage and origin. His favorite etymological resonance was between *sophia* (wisdom) and *sophrosyne* (temperance, restraint). He was forever preaching the necessity of *sophrosyne* as the foundation of sophia.

It was often said by the Orphics, and provable by anyone who engages the process of harmonic temperance, that as the personal and inter-personal *harmonia* grows, the *harmonia* of the kosmos can be heard and enjoyed. *Sophrosyne* is certainly the foundation of *sophia*.

The Orphic description of maturation clearly asserted the necessity for restraint in the attunement to harmonia. But let it be noted: While tuning the strings of the lyre involves much tightening, the ideal is neither too loose nor too tight. Or in the wise (and Sokratic) words of Mae West, "I'm all for restraint, so long as it doesn't go too far."

Understanding Sublime

At the peak of a heritage tree, surveying and assessing the Tennessee landscape I knew well as a young walker, I wondered why the word "understanding" wasn't "overstanding", since when I "got it" or comprehended something, I seemed to be taking an overview, a heightened recognition of an embedded pattern.

Well in fact, there was a Middle English word *overstonden*, literally "overstand." But *overstonden* was used only in literal, actual, physical circumstances, as if you were describing someone upon a tree limb or balcony. Conversely, the person standing below you in the creek would be described by *undergestandan*.

My confusion was at last resolved when I learned that there are two "under"'s. "Under", as in "below", we get from the Germanic *unter*, "below", PIE *ndher-*, "under". Amazingly, this appears to be a completely different root from the "under" of understanding. The connotation of the Old English *under-* in "understanding" is *within*, not below. Indeed, as we look deeper still, we find that the *under-* of understanding has its PIE deep root in *nter-*, "between, among", as evidenced by the Sanskrit *antar* and the Latin and English *inter*, all meaning "between" and "among".

In fact, there was an Old English word *understandan*, meaning comprehension, and it is literally translated as "stand in the midst of." To be true to its deepest roots and our current conventions and meaning, "understanding" would be better written as *interstanding*. Walk a mile in my shoes, within my life, among my sensations, to understand/interstand my world, so says native wisdom.

However, before I came to this *interstanding*, I held a hierarchical sensitivity, especially to certain downward subjects. "Subject" is the Latin *sub-* "under" with *iacere*, "to throw.") Being subject to the king in 13th century Europe was followed by certain 14th century people who described their subjective feeling as recipients of actions. Two hundred years later at the re-birth (Re-naissance) of Hellenic philosophy, the phrase *subject matter* appeared, borrowed from the Latin, *subjecta materia*. This was in turn taken from Aristotle's *hypokeimene hyle*, literally "that which lives or lies beneath", my favorite subject.

With my heightened interest in downward subjects, I came to learn how the Underworld is the dominion of Hades, and how this name is from *a-des*, not day, un-conscious. But once you have turned over your unconscious Hades sufficiently, you learn a new name for the underground divinity: *Pluto*, the divinity of riches. For beneath the soil, jewels and precious metals are found.

For when an unconscious pattern is revealed, harvested, and polished, an unhappiness is converted to a sensitivity and richness of feeling. Thus it is said, "Where you stumble, there's where you find your treasure." This Hades to Pluto transition is the prayer of every soul.

In the midst of this transition, sometimes I feel like I am forever turning the ground; sometimes I am forever lying in that rich plowed field.

As we are restored to joy, we find ourselves within a rich beauty; this is understanding indeed, and in truth. We surrender within this beauteous reality and sublimities bless the being.

Surrender is an Old French word meaning "deliver over, give up," as *sur* is not a French version the Latin *sub*, but a French rendering of the Germanic *super*, "over". *Render* is the French for "give", from the Latin *dare*, "to give", with its deepest root in the PIE *da*, "give". Surrender is a total giving over.

Giving your self over completely is anathema or suspicious in today's world of achievement, success, and independence. The fear that *sending* one's head *down* in true *submission* leads to being *yoked under* or *subjugation* is grounded in reality, for the past is replete with such abuse. Instead, with wide eyes we must discern what and who we give ourselves to and then grow in our giving. Grounded in continual discernment, our surrender flows without withholding and we find ourselves within "the secret women's mysteries" that allows anyone to be lifted "up to" (Old French *sub-*) and beyond the limits of the threshold (*limen*) to the lofty sublime.

How do we arrive in the life where sublimities bless the heart and understanding quiets the mind? All the traditions agree: We must *stand below* our self-oriented conventions in the ground of real existence; we must be people of *substance*.

Human

"Human" shares etymological ground with "humus", rich earth (in Hebrew, *adam*). We humans, like countless living things before us and with us, grow out of fecund soil upwards towards the light.

However, our down-to-earth view rarely sees the true horizon of our possibility, and in modern times is downright incredulous about the voice of the supposed "other" race of beings, those not "human", not of earth ascending upwards, but the gods and the race of the descended Beings ("down-crossing" = *ava-tara*). Distinctively different from common and even extraordinary women and men, these rarest of people are described as fully conscious and freely feeling, the pure, the Heaven Born, the virgin-birthed, the God-descended-One, Avatars, the Divine Person Incarnate, Enlightened Love Incarnate.

It has been often reported that these "unborn" Ones took on an ordinary-looking form in order to teach the Way of Truth and demonstrate the very Heart to us self-oriented, dirty humans. These coming-down servants stand at the root of most of the world's religions.

The Bhagavad Gita sings Krishna's words with immortal nectar. "When righteousness declines and there is no love, I assume the form of man and I rise again. But I am not born and I shall never die."

Avatar Adi Da states self-evidently, "Spiritually Realized Adepts (or Transmission-Masters, or True Gurus) are the principal Sources, Resources, and Means of the esoteric (or Spiritual) Way. This fact is not (and never has been) a matter of controversy among real Spiritual practitioners."

Strikingly, it is reported that to simply be in the Company of these "Transmission-Masters" was/is considered sufficient to mature in perfect happiness. The core of these religions was not found in a set of ideas, but in felt relationship with the Incarnation.

The Master-devotee relationship is particularly difficult for the modern mind, immersed in egalitarian, abstract, and worldly presumptions. For membership in the "human" race is supposed to be of the earth growing upward. We may accept a prophet or messenger of God, but "the Mouth of God" seems heretical, doesn't it?

Heresy

In a convoluted evolution, "heresy" ended right up there with "wrong". But it didn't start out that way. It is rooted in the Hellenic *aireo*, to take with your hand, to grasp. This evolved into *airesis*, choice, election. Thus, new ideas could be chosen, ever-new schools of thought could be grasped and elected.

This was revolutionary. By the first century of the Common Era, Diodorus of Sicily complained that the Hellenes, in contrast to the peoples East, always felt free to choose a new doctrinal innovation in important matters, freely grasping a new *hairesis* [the "h" is how English demarcates an aspirated *ai*]. By the second century, *hairesis* had become a standard term to indicate distinct philosophical schools.

However, in the fourth century, the Council at Nicaea canonized the Christian Scripture and with Imperial power soon purged all other knowledge as false beliefs or heresy. Freely choosing new ideas was bitten by the dogma. Who's heretical now?

Iota

The "i" or iota, is the smallest letter in the Greek alphabet. But this tiniest of demarcations took center stage at the first great Council of Nicaea in 325. Constantine, after his conversion to Christianity, noticed there were many, many kinds of Christianity across his empire and he commissioned a council to have then unified and clarified — and put into one book.

At Nicaea, there were hundreds of representatives of the various Christian sects from all across the Mediterranean, and there were hundreds of chapters vying to be placed in the Book (Greek: *Biblio*).

One prominent requirement for inclusion in the Book was that it must be usable by everyone, from the common people to the sophisticate. However, being universally accessible meant that some erudite books, as well as all controversial accounts and gnostic or esoteric knowledge would not be included. ("Universal" is the Latin translation of the Hellenic *kata-holon*, literally "down from the whole".) The Bible must be universal, they insisted, even if some nuances and subtleties are lost. Such is the origin of that *catholic* requirement.

(After the Council, these controversial and esoteric scrolls were declared heretical and received such scorn and persecution from the Catholic Church that many had to be hidden back at home. Some waited millennia to be found, e.g. The Dead Sea Scrolls.)

But the most controversial point of the Council concerned the distinction between inspired humans and divine incarnations. Was Jesus (Greek for *Joshua*) descended from God or a God-infused, but human-prophet? Was Joshua, son of Mary from Galilee, the messenger of God or the mouth of God?

The protagonists were Athanasios (Mouth of God) and Arius (messenger of God). The Arian argument went something like: Jesus was a human, and no matter how much God infused him, the limitations in the structure of being human would dictate that he be considered similar to God, inspired by God, full of God, taken over by God even, but not God Himself.

Athanasios replied with certainty. The ancients agree: God can do whatever He wants; if the Divine Presence that is the ground of everything and everyone wants to take form and be born, then that is no problem; the Infinite is not critically qualified by the finite. Period. The principle of avataric incarnation has always been found in great teachings. The Nazarene was not similar, he was the Same.

The words they used to describe "similar presence" and "same presence" are *homoiousia* and *homoousia*, differentiated only by the little "i". (Also translatable as "similar essence" and "same essence" or "similar substance" and "same substance".)

But at last, the intense argument over the iota ended with a ballot. The Council voted overwhelmingly (~300 to 2) for *homoousia*, the "Same", stating that there was not an iota of difference between Jesus and the presence and substance of

God. This is why the Nicene Creed says, "God of God, Light of Light, very God of very God, begotten, not made. Being of one substance with the Father..."

Unfortunately, childish interpretation of these words spoils them with provincial exclusivity. Immature exegesis is a problem in every religion and province, whereas the substance and ground is the Same in all.

Every time you hear the words "not an iota of difference" you can recall how the ancient way of simple relationship with the Incarnation or Avatar has been revered around the world.

Heart Feeling

The PIE *kerd-* is the shared root of the Latin and English *core*, the Hellenic *cardia*, the Hindi *hri-dayam* (heart), the German *herz*, and the English *heart*. Because they share the same root, the two English words "core" and "heart" hold great equivalence and can be used to define each other. The "core" and the "heart" of something or someone are one and the same.

The core or heart of a person can be referring to their cardiac organ or to feeling or the spirit or deepest ground. This dimensionality reflects the spiritual teachings on the three kinds of love: *eros*, *agape*, and *divine*. Eros includes the mundane (I love baseball) and the romantic. The sense of promise for a fuller self is the signature desire of eros. Agape is the love that is signed by giving and self-transcendence. It's often what we call, "real love" as opposed to romance. Agape itself matures beyond the matrices of appearances to the love of the divine, the Condition of all conditions, the very heart of existence.

We know about the heart of the body via the touch of science. We know about the three loves because it is said that we "feel" love. Like the kinds of love and three hearts, we find that the word "feeling" has many implications and a core conveyance.

Looking backwards in time, we find "I feel like I want to" in the early part of the 19th century; one hundred years earlier "feeling" was used to describe "a sensation produced by something". As modern English began to congeal in the late 16th century, "feeling" carried a sense of sympathy and compassion. In the 15th century, "feeling" included your opinion or "how you feel about something". In the 14th century, "feeling" was used to describe an emotion (e-motion: that which moves us). In the 13th century, "feeling" conveyed the sense of being conscious of a sensation or emotion, while the late 12th century "feeling" was used to describe the sense of touch. The Old English *felan* likewise meant to touch, but also "to perceive through senses which are not referred to by any special organ." If we go back through the Proto-Germanic *foljan*, we ultimately come to the PIE root *pal-* "to touch".

Feeling is the sensation of connection, whether physical, emotional, or spiritual. As a surgeon or student, we can feel the smooth muscles of the heart as we touch the organ; as social animals, we can feel our opinion and sense the feelings of others, especially our pals; our limbic brains can sense or feel emotions; our higher brains can feel the discernment of the three hearts and kinds of love; our spirit can touch or feel our very core. Feeling is the sensation of connection, the consciousness of the body, and is present in multi-dimensional ways.

We grow or mature in feeling; we grow to include all the kinds of love; we mature from animal/physical to emotional to sympathy to spirit. We feel, we touch, the heart, our core.

Get Real?

The Vedas are similar to many other pre-historic tales with their mythological stories explaining humanity's common experience and conveying essential wisdoms. They are all idealistic in their descriptions and prescriptions.

The historical fulfillment (ontology, *-anta*) of the Vedas is called *Vedanta*, present as the first critical or realistic scripture, the Upanishads. "Upanishads" literally refers to the teaching received "at the feet of" an avatar or enlightened guru. Instead of having people believe in a host of mythological characters and prescriptions, these Upanishadic gurus demanded that their students undertake a thorough and deep self-examination. The refrain "from the unreal to the Real" peals penetratingly throughout the principal Upanishads.

The word "real" holds great meaning; indeed, it could be said that meaning itself is purposed to or grounded in what is real. Most meaningful is most real.

The contemplation of the etymology of "real" sheds significant light. "Real" is founded in the Latin *res*, thing, root of our "reification", making a thing, thingness. In common linguistic parlance, "real" basically means you can touch it.

Via this etymological examination, we find evidence of a fundamental linguistic slant: all languages are rooted in the physical: doesn't this make *sense*? Can you see how the myopia of language refracts thought through the somatic lens? And since we think via thoughts, shouldn't this objectifying, physical, sensual slant of language be appreciated in our understanding to what is most "real"?

For "real" connotes far more than the somatic, "real" is more than earth, and indeed more than sky, more than emotional, prior to the abstract, subtler than the subtle, more than anything and everything that changes; "real" really indicates what is most fundamental, the ground of being itself.

"Those who see the truth of things acknowledge that whatever exists eternally never changes, and whatever does not exist eternally only changes. Such seers of truth also realize that the entire realm of change, even the body-mind and even the soul itself, is pervaded, each and all, by That which exists eternally." – Bhagavad Gita

More than the concrete or somatic slant that language prefers, and even more than what is entirely the case, really "real" points to the Ground of Being itself: that which is always and already the case, not created or destroyed. Reflected in the fundamental laws of thermodynamics, this fundamental truth of existence includes both object and subject, beyond and including the body-mind complex and the world. It is the myopia of the body-mind that makes subjective and objective, make awareness "in" and energy/matter "out". When the tensing that makes "I" is undone, being overwhelms the knot of self and world in the glory of immortal feeling. For real.

Truth

Baseball players and carpenters know what it means to declare a certain piece of wood "true". It is firm, straight, and resonant. In fact, the Germanic words "true", "tree", and "trust" share a common root in the PIE root *deru-* "to be firm, solid, steadfast".

But "truth" is more than merely steadfastly or resonantly true. The original western conception of Truth was not cast by the German philosophers (full disclosure: Heidegger was my first philosophical love), but by our Hellenic founders.

Where Germanic English says "truth", the Hellenes utter "alethia". But to feel or understand what the philosophers of Hellas meant by "alethia" is not easy. To glimpse alethia's truth involves Orpheus' trip to the Underworld, a too-brief survey of original philosophy, and the awareness that is greater than self and death.

It was said that a spiritual master named Orpheus went through the Underworld, saw the after-death realms, and conveyed that story and its wisdom to humankind. According to him, when you died you were possessed by an extreme thirst. It was the sum total of all the things you wished for, hoped for, thirsted for while alive.

First, the newly dead are first judged on how well they kept their oaths (*juris*) and promises. Next, the parched psyches come upon the Pool of Lethe, the waters of forgetfulness, the drink of unconsciousness. (*Lethe* is the root of our "lethargic" and "lethal".) Most fall upon the waters and satisfy themselves in the lethargy of oblivion, but then they wander without end in the grey flatlands of Asphodel.

But those who had been initiated into the mysteries and took up a life of spiritual practice knew to not settle for the first satisfaction that appears. Indeed, when presented with what seems to be an easy solution, they use that *siren* (lit. "binding") call as the signal to look up. Initiated souls trained during life by metanoia know to turn their vision up from the self-satisfaction of forgetfulness and to the vision of a white tree that appears in blessing.

Going the way of the white tree, blessed souls find another pool, the waters of Remembrance, *Mnemnosyne* (root of our "memory"). Genuflecting to drink these immortal nectars, one's thirst is truly quenched.

The "secret women's mysteries" appear in the submission to joy. One is washed in the transmission of communion, "like a thirsty kid who has fallen into milk." Via communion, one enters the Fields of Elysium with its eternal celebration. Via communion comes union and Orphic "self-realization".

Orpheus' description of the immortal process of spiritual realization is confluent with yogic analyses of esoteric processes. Indeed, we learn to turn from temporary pleasures to longer lasting ones, from mere satisfactions of the flesh to the celebration of relationship. The *harmonia* that this temperance yields has rising tones of more and more wonderful tunings, until the harmony engendered by one's restraint is resonant with the *harmonia* of the *kosmos*. Nectars within the brain are signalled by these higher tones and ooze their feeling of supreme being, overflowing the "crater of the head". When your cup runneth over, this was called *Stephanos*, the nectar of truth, the overflowing crown of heart-joy.

Orpheus' theological understanding of reality was conveyed to the later philosophers. *Lethe* was covered-ness and forgetfulness, while its opposite, *alethia*, was the revealing and remembered truth. *Alethia, a-lethia, a-lethe*, not Lethe, not lethargic, not covered or forgetful -- *alethia*, revelatory Truth. Truth is initiated as one looks up from the ephemeral pool of driven-self-obsession.

It was Parmenides (fl. 500-460 B.C.E.) who shouted *aletheia*. But an extremely brief survey of original Hellenic philosophy shows the context of that exclamation.

According to Aristotle et al, it was Thales (fl 600-546 B.C.E.) who first spoke philosophically/scientifically about reality, without the poesy of myth or the rhapsody of theology. Thales did not repeat the Orphic original egg theory, nor any mythological construct, nor did he stitch a flow of words together rhapsodically. Instead, he proposed prosaically that water must be at the origin of all things. Without water, there is no life.

Thales' younger friend Anaximander also took up the new prosaic way of speaking, but he proposed that the "unbounded" was at the root of everything. He was followed by Anaximenes (d. 528 B.C.E.) who said that there had to be something there, perhaps air. Xenophanes (d. 475 B.C.E.) then exclaimed that the unbounded infinite is not only at the root of all things, but is the very substance of all and All. Parmenides came along and asked, "Who cares what is the archetype? What is reality? What is the truth? How can we come to this *alethia*?" [Sokrates followed him and had a similar break with archetypal concerns. "If you will simply take care of your psyche, take care of your soul, your feeling being, then all these questions will be naturally resolved."]

Parmenides' *Alethia* or Truth, in this original regard, was in no way limited to the factual or material; the implication of *alethia* resonated with the Orphic and mystic descriptions: *alethia* was closer to conscious understanding, noble being, remembrance, divine revelation, and paradise. In this exalted sense, *alethia* describes the truth of reality as what is, when we have worked to remove all the coverings.

Alethia's uncovered, un-forgetful, un-lazy quality bespeaks of the wise ones who look up from themselves, who look up from the lethargic pool of lethal self-satisfaction and see and feel the radiance of primal light in everything and thus the truth in everyone.

To engage the truth is very specifically not lazy. The spiritual process dedicated to the truth works every moment to un-cover, look up, and remember the perfect relatedness and glorious singularity of real existence. Understanding the lethargic underworld and understanding the immortal worlds is just a metaphor for understanding the real truth of existence now.

Part II

The Error of Belief

When people ask if I believe in God, I ask them if they believe in beauty. By answering their question with a (telling) question, I attempt to initiate an inquiry into the trouble with the word "believe", along with its nominative form, "belief".

While manifest beauty may be subtle and ephemeral, beauty is not something you believe in — in order to experience it. We naturally see beauty, hear beautiful sounds, intercourse with beautiful smells and touches, even feel beauteous. We don't "believe" in beauty, just like we don't "believe" in gravity or not. Belief is not the method whereby we intercourse with beauty or gravity. In contrast, "God" (the Abrahamic theological word for the fundamental Reality or beauteous "divinity") has become something that we "believe" in or not.

Yet beauty and God are at least related, if not identical. Do you have to believe in beauty to experience beauty? No, it's self-evident. Belief is not required in order for us to be informed by the beautiful.

Former nun and renown scholar Karen Armstrong has called our use of the words belief/believe "a cul-de-sac of history", wherein our social dialogue is stuck going round and round. *"The extraordinary and eccentric emphasis on "belief" in Christianity today is an accident of history that has distorted our understanding of religious truth. We call religious people "believers", as though acceptance of a set of doctrines was their principal activity, and before undertaking the religious life many feel obliged to satisfy themselves about the metaphysical claims of the church, which cannot be proven rationally since they lie beyond the reach of empirical sense data."*

As a result of this "accident of history", our modern attempt to privatize our "beliefs" is going nowhere and to engage the dramatic discussion surrounding the orthodoxies of provincial belief and scientific materialism is dizzying. Therefore, it behooves us to understand this error of belief, this accident of history, so that we can see our way forward.

Albert Einstein pointed out that many problems cannot be solved by the level of awareness that created them. So rather than arguing about the validity of our beliefs, let's look closely what belief is, where it came from, what it is attempting to do, and how to transform the dead end of our private beliefs into widespread understanding.

•••••

An academic examination of the historical use of the words belief/believe will shed light how "belief" came to mean what it does in today's conversation.

"Belief/believe" can be traced back to the Old English *geleafa*, "to hold dear" (*ge-* changed to *be-* in the late 12C). Deeper roots can be found in the Proto-Indo-Euro root *leub*, meaning "care, desire, love". The English word "love" is from the Germanic *lieb*, related to *leafa* and *leub*. "Believe" is quite close to "beloved" as they share the same root of love.

Coming out of the Dark ages with the nascent re-birth of rational, scientific views, some of the teachings and "beliefs" of the Christian Church were questioned and a long-running conflict ensued. In the late 12th century, (Saint) Anselm attempted to construct a scientific proof of the existence of God and bring peace to the growing friction. Beginning in the 13th century, "belief" had a religious sense as things true as a matter of religious doctrine. By the 16th century, "belief" had become limited to "mental acceptance of something as true." The battle between science and religion seemed endless.

Based on meticulous, long-term observations, Copernicus mathematically justified "the revolution of celestial spheres" which was only mildly opposed by the Church. A generation later, one of the Church's own Dominican friars, Giordano Bruno, went even further than the heliocentricity of Copernicus and proposed that the sun is probably just another ordinary star among the countless stars and that many, many stars probably have planets, and that some of them must be worlds like ours with intelligent beings like us. Well, this of course, was utterly unacceptable to the mighty Church's "only begotten son/chosen people" mentality. The Roman Inquisition burned their own open-minded, highly intelligent and deeply devoted friar at the stake in 1600 and then went after Galileo and Tyche. The backlash was strong: the Church had not enforced its power, but lost potency, suffered great shame, and a peace was invoked.

"Belief", as we now use it, was born in that early 17th century truce. It was a compromise word, so that the social dialogue around provincial religion and modernist science can agree not to kill each other. "Well, it's my belief that..." is how we often preface our statements, and even science is "believed" or not.

But this only dances around a faux armistice while the war goes on. May Giordano Bruno's death not be in vain. We need to take the next step out of the conflict. We need to understand our error thoroughly and gracefully grow in the understanding that is already at peace.

•••••

"Belief" holds its social gravity because it is how two words are usually translated: the Biblical Greek *pistis* (and all of its linguistic variations) and also the Church Latin *credo* (with all of it Romantic extensions).

Let us start with the Greek *pistis*. We need to look no further that John 3:16, "God so loved the world that He gave His only begotten son that whoever believes in him so not perish, but have everlasting life."

Pistis is also translated as "faith", as in Matthew 6:30: "If God clothes the fields today (even if tomorrow the grasses are thrown into a furnace), thus He will clothe you, will He not? O you of little faith."

Upon the vast tree of language, *pistis* and

"faith/fidelity" interestingly share the same deep, Proto-Indo-Euro root *bheid*, "to be awake/aware" (also root of "Buddha"). But "belief" and "faith" are poor (or narrow) translations of *pistis*. The Liddell and Scott Greek Lexicon reveals that *pistis* is used to indicate "trust in others, the feeling of assurance, confidence, good faith, and honesty". An aware, honest sense of trust is the dominant meaning conveyed by *pistis*. [There are many, many uses of *pistis* (tr. as "faith" and "belief") in the Christian scripture that can be re-appreciated and even re-translated into this deeper trust and confident awareness.] *Pistis* is not the suspension of discernment but the assurance that comes with glimpsing what is not limited by time.

In ancient Greece Pistis was a spirit, a personification of trust, faith, and reliability. Because people need/use images, parables, and stories to support their understanding, it was said that the spirit Pistis surrounded and aided honest and harmonious people—along with her companions Elpis (Hope), Sophrosyne (Temperance), and Charites (the Graces). (Pistis' Roman equivalent was Fides, Fidelity, Faith).

The Latin *credo* is also translated as "I believe". We need to look no further than the refrain of the Nicene Creed: "We believe in one God, the Father Almighty, Maker of all things visible and invisible; We believe in Jesus Anointed, having the same Being as the Father ..." Worthy to note is that *credo* has a deep root in the Proto-Indo-Euro, *kerd-dhe*, "to put one's heart" (into something). As has been pointed out, *kerd* can be heard in the Greek word for heart, *kardia*; in the

Latin word for heart, core; in the Sanskrit, *hri-dayam*; and in the Germanic *herz* and the English *heart*. "Believe" and "creed", like love and heart, are obviously related.

It was the war between religion and science that twisted the Church Latin *credo* and the original Hellenic *pistis* into "faith" and "belief" and "belief" into something for which there is no proof. And that twist of abstraction gave us orthodoxy (with its repression) and the privatization of understanding—even as its bent took away the deeper resonances of real trust.

Pistis used to mean "trust in absolute or fundamental reality, trust in supreme being, trust in the divine beauty", and among the Abrahamic religions (Judaism, Christianity, Islam), "trust in God".

Faith conveyed a "loyalty to a person based on promise or duty". "Keep good faith" has been common advice for centuries. Faith, as cognate of Latin fides, also took on its religious sense beginning in 14 century. And by the 17th century, "belief" was reduced to the un-provable conviction and "faith" was your confidence in God and your church. Science marched forward and gained power, but abstraction's weakness in alienation and manipulation was regularly met by emotional "great awakenings". The incompleteness of science and the immaturity of official churches caused the war to rage on.

••••

"Belief" was cast as a mockery upon the stage of

modernity's flatland. In *Through the Looking-Glass* the White Queen says, "Why, sometimes I've believed as many as six impossible things before breakfast." All beliefs would soon be explained as a compensation for psychological immaturity. Certainly this can be true. But while early understanding has serious developmental and provincial limitations, there is truth conveyed by all the religions and a simple relationship to these provincial frameworks of truth helps us grow (and maintain social stability).

Mature consideration of the nature of language, thought, and understanding is rare and it is obvious that beliefs serve a great function in providing basic wisdoms for good-hearted people. Of course in a single world of one very large family, different ways of living and looking at realities will take a bit of time; this we have noticed.

The integration of science and religion is not only possible; it is the next step we are taking. Have you heard the good news? Everything is a form of light. You just have to change your way of looking at things and suddenly the estate of heaven is at hand.

Via the 20th century dominance of scientific everyman/woman, our intuition of fundamental reality was pushed into inwardness and psychology. Personal opinion was now sacrosanct along with personal beliefs. But it is commonly said, "opinions are like assholes, every body has one". Suddenly, the privatization of beliefs and opinion reduces what is deeply useful to the heart to the level of feces. Being reduced or confined to provincial beliefs can stink up our sense of our deepest reality.

Perhaps that is too harsh. After all, millions of people get great solace and wisdom from their beliefs. That is good and carries great truth, but the problems begin when we bring what is true and wonderful from the personal to the widely shared. The provinces have blossomed beyond their origins into a new world, but are having a hard time adjusting their language of absolutes with others. Poignantly, we must hear and heed the call of the prophets and not demand our provincial interpretation be the only face or name of the faceless and nameless divinity.

Intuiting the unconditional foundation of all conditions, we can understand that human knowledge is forever small compared to the whole of reality, and trust in what is beyond all human understanding, in what is unlimited, unconditional, wholly foundational, most real. We can humbly align ourselves to the truth we glimpse in scientific revelation as well as in sacred words from every province. Right action, right practice, or orthopraxy is how we align ourselves to the fullest truth, not the "straight opinion" or orthodoxy of belief. We must understand scripture in depth, not just believe it: that is how we show its truth. We walk the walk, not just talk the talk. To fully understand love, we must not only be loved, we must actively love. Therefore, to merely "believe" in scripture is, at depth, a heresy.

•••••

There are positive uses and implications in the word "belief". It does suggest the engaged trust of *pistis*, not just orthodoxy. "Belief" is oriented to the feeling core or creed, rather than the abstraction of knowledge. "Belief" intimates the trust in what is beyond knowledge or human understanding, and affords a rightful humility. For however powerful and responsible we may grow to be, reality is unlimited and unfathomable at last. "Belief" suggests that self-knowledge and 'divine' appreciation.

But unless we are specific and intentional in the use of the word "belief", the stink of orthodoxy creeps in like the flatulence of the common arrogance.

•••••

In ancient Hellas, it was observed that there were two ways to interpret sacred story. The *demotiki*, or common people, took the stories to have literal truth, but the sophisticated knew the stories in their *ouranos* (heavenly), metaphorical sense. Accordingly, two methods of understanding were appreciated: *mythos* and *logos*, story and reason.

Now there are many ways in which reason has surpassed and bested myth, story, and legend. But we must also appreciate that there are times when a story best conveys an idea, and is able to convey it widely. Beyond the aetiological or explanatory myths, *mythos* provides understanding of the human situation in two very useful ways.

One, *mythos* intimates the invisible dimension of reality where the spirit of the individual's behavior, reciprocity, and prayerful intention show mysterious intercourse. Two, *mythos* provides a primary psychology. From Oedipus and Electra to Narcissus and Psyche, from King Midas and Medusa to the stages of Dionysus, deep human issues are given a framework for understanding and growth.

In *ouranos* and metaphorical light, *logos* appreciates *mythos*, and sees how both *mythos* and *logos* are useful to understanding and have overlapping domains of influence. For instance: it is thoroughly logical to love all the time, but how's that going for you?

What is more helpful than reasonable conclusions is to understand our primary psychology, especially those depicted in mythos. See how you are self-possessed and self-fascinated like Narcissus, or act out unconscious patterns because of your father and mother, O Oedipus and Electra. Do you confuse the happiness of things with the happiness of relationship like Midas? Or does your hubris transform even your beauty into a head of snakes? Will your Psyche trust Love at last and drink Zeus' immortal ambrosia? *Mythos* trumps *Logos* in usefulness in places.

But even the *demotiki*, the common people who operated in the concrete/literal sense, did not "believe" the mythos to be so true that another version of the telling was wrong. Many versions of the same myth did not indicate falsity, but subtlety. (Look at the ancient Hebrews and their five stories of creation in *Genesis*.) Stories were indicators, reflections, a way to sufficiently understand so that you may live rightly; mythos was neither fact nor proposals to be merely believed. The point is right living, not right opinion. You learn this by right living, not by thinking about the rulebook. Even the *demotiki* knew this in the ancient world.

But today, the scientific framework has so thoroughly destroyed the credulity of *mythos* that now logic is the only path to truth. "That's a myth" means "it's not true." Certainly, *logos* participates in reality, but so does *mythos*. And while *logos* is superior in many ways, there are places where mythos helps us better and we can come to a renewed appreciation of the functions of myth, such as proposed by Joseph Campbell and the like.

But more importantly, we must discern where (and how) *logos* is useful, where (and how) *mythos* is useful; where we think and ponder where we trust our gut; where we formulate knowledge and where we stand in awe. Let us jettison "belief" from the precinct of our deep knowledge and sacred intuition and turn from this error of private belief to our single human family with its world of wisdom.

Our use of the word "belief" and "believe" must be tempered and made conscious. Instead of "my beliefs", we can say, "It is my understanding…" Or where it fits, "belief" can be replaced with "trust" or "faith". I can still believe in my students and fellows, have faith that they will persevere in growing beyond themselves in tolerance and cooperation, open-mindedness and mutual appreciation. I believe we can grow beyond orthodoxy to right practice, and I understand that change is the real truth.

We can exit whatever cul-de-sac we are in and turn every sword in the war between science and religion into a plowshare. We don't believe in divine beauty; we stand in awe of beauty and the unconditional reality, through all of its conditional forms. And we trust in that reality which we behold.

Epilogue: Heraklitos Redux

"If you have not heard me by all of this but Logos,
then I can say: All is One."

Also by Frank Marrero

Lincoln Beachey: The Man Who Owned the Sky

The Recollection of Sokrates

Big Philosophy for Little Kids: Writing with Character

The Superpowers of Fasting: Ancient Arts and Medical Miracles

The View from Delphi: Rhapsodies of Hellenic Wisdom and an Ecstatic Appreciation of Western History

A Monkey's Tale for the Divine Person: Leelas in Praise of Avatar Adi Da Samraj

forthcoming

Telling Fish About Water: On the Process of Perception and Seeing the Truth

The Early Life Adventures of Frankie Free Boy: Naive Tales from a Most Ridiculous Life

www.frankmarrero.com

About the Author

Frank Marrero lives just north of San Francisco's Golden Gate and teaches elementary children in inner city schools. He is the proud father of Ella (17) and Salem (21), and loves to fast, hike, and write.

In his native Tennessee, Frank first encountered Adi Da in 1976 and two years later, just after his 26th birthday, Frank sold his businesses and home to live near Adi Da. Adi Da brought Frank into his intimate sphere, blessing Frank with fiery illuminations and nectarous sublimities.

Adi Da's enlightened company baptised Frank in the heart of being, so that all thought bows to the heart's truth. May you find Adi Da's imprint and heart-insistence throughout this text.

Adi Da also charged Frank to study the pre-Socratic mystery traditions for a decade and write about it. This passion continues as his life's work.

Adi Da left, Frank Marrero, right, Hawaii, 1982

www.ingramcontent.com/pod-product-compliance
Lightning Source LLC
Chambersburg PA
CBHW031424040426
42444CB00006B/696